# COTTAGERS AND INDIANS

## ALSO BY DREW HAYDEN TAYLOR

# COTTAGERS
## AND INDIANS

A PLAY BY

Drew Hayden Taylor

with an afterword by
Leanne Betasamosake Simpson

Talonbooks

Talonbooks
9259 Shaughnessy Street, Vancouver, British Columbia, Canada v6p 6r4
talonbooks.com

Talonbooks is located on xʷməθkʷəy̓əm, Sḵwx̱wú7mesh, and səl̓ilwətaʔɬ Lands.

Fifth printing: 2021

Typeset in Arno
Printed and bound in Canada on 100% post-consumer recycled paper

Cover and interior design by Typesmith
Cover photographs of Herbie Barnes and Tracey Hoyt in *Cottagers and Indians* at the Tarragon Theatre, Toronto, February–March 2018, by Cylla von Tiedemann

Talonbooks acknowledges the financial support of the Canada Council for the Arts, the Government of Canada through the Canada Book Fund, and the Province of British Columbia through the British Columbia Arts Council and the Book Publishing Tax Credit.

Canada Council   Conseil des arts
for the Arts     du Canada

BRITISH
COLUMBIA

BRITISH COLUMBIA
ARTS COUNCIL
An agency of the Province of British Columbia

Rights to produce *Cottagers and Indians,* in whole or in part, in any medium by any group, amateur or professional, are retained by the author. Interested persons are requested to contact Janine Cheeseman, Aurora Artists Agency, 19 Wroxeter Avenue, Toronto, Ontario, m4k 1j5; telephone: 416-463-4634; fax: 416-463-4889; email: aurora.artists@sympatico.ca.

library and archives canada cataloguing in publication

Taylor, Drew Hayden, 1962–, author

    Cottagers and Indians : a play / Drew Hayden Taylor ; with an afterword by Leanne Betasamosake Simpson.

isbn 978-1-77201-230-9 (softcover)

    i. Simpson, Leanne Betasamosake, 1971–, writer of afterword ii. Title.

ps8589.a885c68 2019        c812'.54        c2018-905729-7

*I would like to dedicate this book to James Whetung and the Save Pigeon Lake people for contributing so much to Canada's Indigenous theatre development.*

# PLAYWRIGHT'S PREFACE

This is the little play about *manoomin* (wild rice) that could, to paraphrase a children's book. This is not a work I had planned to write. It wasn't on my radar. It wasn't tickling my cerebellum demanding to burst forth and take shape. Yet oddly enough, I was surrounded by the topic and its potential. I even wrote an article several years back for Toronto's *NOW Magazine* detailing the issues involved. It took an out-of-the-blue email from Tarragon Theatre Artistic Director Richard Rose to physically point me toward the obvious. He had read a different article about the issue, that is to say a bizarre disagreement between James Whetung, rogue Anishnawbe wild rice entrepreneur and food sovereigntist, and some disgruntled local cottagers. The issue – James's ongoing plan to restock *manoomin* in the Kawartha Lakes, where it grew and thrived prior to the advancement of "civilization."

Normally you would think this would not be a problem to result in several years of conflict, media articles, news interviews, and eventually a play. But you see when *manoomin* matures, it stands sometimes a good thirty to sixty centimetres above the waterline. According to various cottagers, it hampers swimming, fishing, boating, and property values – all precious assets of the comfortable cottage summer. Thus the conflict. Things got ugly and clashes persisted for several years. Still today there is the occasional spat between the two sides.

My first draft was a one-man show, completely from Arthur Copper's perspective. I'd never written a one-person show before and this seemed like a natural. But alas, it seemed immediately obvious Arthur needed a foil to do battle with. Enter Ms. Maureen Poole, champion of the Muskoka chair warriors. The rest, as they say, is history.

At first, I wasn't sure if a play about differing attitudes toward a half-wild, half-cultivated grain would garner any reaction. Yes there was plenty of conflict, but enough to make people leave the comfort of their homes and pay good money for seats in order to pretend to be out on the Kawartha Lakes? I tried to present both sides fairly ... as fairly as I could. Admittedly, I have known James forever. I went to school with several of his brothers and sisters, and I like the gentleman. But after having lived several years in Toronto, I can safely say some of my best friends are cottagers. So there you go.

In the end the play ran for almost five weeks, with each week getting stronger and stronger audiences. For obvious reasons, the vast majority were non-Indigenous. But what was interesting to me was the fact that many were cottagers themselves, seemingly very supportive of James's battle. There was the odd one who would tell a friend or two of mine who were scattered in the audience that they were there to see what my perspective was. Let's face it, the vast majority of cottage owners no doubt come from the Greater Toronto Area. This was about them.

The end result ... an unexpected and overwhelming acceptance and appreciation of the show. I could be wrong but it's always appeared to me that my take on theatre and on Indigenous issues themselves is different from most other Indigenous playwrights'. I love to explore and teach through humour. Based on my experiences with other storytellers, it is our way. Yes this play has a lot of anger in it. A lot of history. Even some sadness, but humour is the focal point of much of what happens. I read somewhere that one of the best ways to understand a people is through what makes them laugh. Sounds good to me.

Thank you for coming to visit Arthur and Maureen. In retrospect, they're both single. Maybe in the sequel I'll hook them up. Now that would be funny!

—DREW HAYDEN TAYLOR
Curve Lake First Nation

## PRODUCTION HISTORY

*Cottagers and Indians* was first produced from February 13 to March 25, 2018, by Tarragon Theatre in Toronto, Ontario, with the following cast and crew:

| | |
|---|---|
| **ARTHUR** Copper | Herbie Barnes |
| **MAUREEN** Poole | Tracey Hoyt |
| Direction | Patti Shaughnessy |
| Set design | Robin Fisher |
| Costume design | Sage Paul |
| Lighting design | Nick Andison |
| Sound design | Beau Dixon |
| Stage manager | Jennifer Stobart |
| Alternate stage manager | Debbie Read |
| Anishnawbe language coach | Jonathon Taylor |

## CHARACTERS

ARTHUR Copper, an Indigenous man in his late forties

MAUREEN Poole, a well-to-do non-Indigenous woman in her mid-fifties


## SETTING

There are two universes on the stage: on one side is a typical Ontario cottage environment, preferably a dock with a barbeque and a Muskoka chair. On the other side, a canoe in close proximity to a cattailed and picturesque shoreline.

Herbie Barnes in *Cottagers and Indians* by Drew Hayden Taylor at the Tarragon Theatre, Toronto, February–March 2018. Photo by Cylla von Tiedemann. Used with permission.

Tracey Hoyt in *Cottagers and Indians* by Drew Hayden Taylor at the Tarragon Theatre, Toronto, February–March 2018. Photo by Cylla von Tiedemann. Used with permission.

Herbie Barnes and Tracey Hoyt in *Cottagers and Indians* by Drew Hayden Taylor at the Tarragon Theatre, Toronto, February–March 2018. Photos by Cylla von Tiedemann. Used with permission.

Herbie Barnes and Tracey Hoyt in *Cottagers and Indians* by Drew Hayden Taylor at the Tarragon Theatre, Toronto, February–March 2018. Photos by Cylla von Tiedemann. Used with permission.

Herbie Barnes and Tracey Hoyt in *Cottagers and Indians* by Drew Hayden Taylor at the Tarragon Theatre, Toronto, February–March 2018. Photos by Cylla von Tiedemann. Used with permission.

Herbie Barnes in *Cottagers and Indians* by Drew Hayden Taylor at the Tarragon Theatre, Toronto, February–March 2018. Photo by Cylla von Tiedemann. Used with permission.

# COTTAGERS AND INDIANS

*Lights up on* ARTHUR *Copper sitting
in the canoe. His eyes are closed for a
moment; he is breathing in the wind that
surrounds him. He addresses the audience.*

ARTHUR

Smell that breeze. Everything you need to know about
where you are is hanging right there on the wind. It carries
the entire universe. I can smell the water. I can smell
the plant life. I can even tell a storm is coming. And
somewhere off in the distance, somebody is barbequing.
(*sniffing again*) Chicken. Marinated. In beer. Creemore ...
Pale Ale ... (*laughing at his own joke*) Sometimes I think I
could paddle this entire lake with my eyes closed. Just by
my nose. Not a lot of people can claim that. For instance,
about two kilometres down that shore is a swamp. Over
in the other direction, a golf course. Both very different
aromas. One natural. One not so natural. One of these
days I might actually try that, just letting my nose guide
me the length of this lake. They say the old people could
guide like that. Your eyes can fool you but not your nose.
I guess that's why Indians have such big noses.

*Lights up on* MAUREEN *Poole. She is well-
dressed and seemingly comfortable with the
world, with a sense of earned privilege. She
is looking around her surroundings with
a lovely smile. She is also barbequing.*

MAUREEN

You know, there's nothing quite like a nice glass of chilled Chardonnay, superbly oaked, with some tasty barbequed organic chicken, right after an invigorating game of golf. This is my husband's recipe. He says the beer marinade gives it a nice tang. And I am all about a nice tang. This is ... I think ... the fourth barbeque we've had over the years, since we bought this cottage. Wear and tear I suppose. The feasts my family have had out here ... the potato salad alone could fill in this side of the lake. When we first bought this cottage ... back when music was good, there was nothing but wilderness around here. Now, there's two Tim Hortons! I'm more of a Starbucks girl but God knows how long I'll have to wait before I can ...

ARTHUR

Hey?!

MAUREEN

What?

ARTHUR

Can I have some of your chicken?

MAUREEN

This chicken here?

ARTHUR

Yeah, smells pretty good.

MAUREEN

Sorry, but I didn't think chicken was part of your (*using air quotes*) "traditional diet."

ARTHUR

Fine then. Hey, do you know what goes good with marinated organic barbequed chicken? A nice wild rice casserole. (*faking surprise*) Oh right. Sorry. Never mind.

MAUREEN

You, Mr. Copper, are an ass.

ARTHUR

Oh *miigwech.* I am what the Creator made.

MAUREEN

Well, it seems everybody ... even God ... can have an off day.

ARTHUR

Excuse me, but are you slandering both a member of Canada's Indigenous community *and* their deity?

MAUREEN

No. Just your barber. Now, my husband and I have a lovely condo in North York, but this place ... well, we consider it special. We live in Toronto, but this ... this is our home. My husband, he built this dock. We had to have somebody come in and rebuild it, but that's another story. He put in that fireplace. It was against code and we had to have it redone but still, his heart is in that stone. Justin is the kind of guy I'm sure contractors laugh about down at their bar. But he does try. The first summer we were here, we planted those lilac bushes and look at them now. This is a cottage a family built. Terri-Lynne, my magnificent daughter, lives in the States now and Cameron, my oldest, has his own business in Calgary. But they still find the time to come out here at least once a year. Especially, ever since ...

*MAUREEN pauses, in silence. ARTHUR notices.*

ARTHUR
Your marinated organic barbequed chicken is burning.

*MAUREEN snaps out of it, flipping the chicken.*

MAUREEN
Goddamn it!

ARTHUR
*Aaniin,* my name is Arthur Copper. An ordinary name for an ordinary guy. My spirit name is *Nbi-nini.* It means "man of the water." A couple dozen years ago, I was born in this territory. And that woman, her name is Maureen Poole. Doesn't that name just drip with evil? She owns that split-level ranch. Trust me, no good has ever come from a split-level ranch. Within the boundaries of that manicured lawn, that immaculate flower garden, and tiled patio lives ... during four months of the summer and the odd fall and spring weekend ... a woman who has taken it upon herself to rid the county of both me and my wild

rice. That's what you call it, even though it's not actually rice. It's a grain, but whatever, we Anishnawbe call it *manoomin*. Any of you scientist type people, or people who for some reason speak Latin, it's also called *Zizania*. In our language, *manoomin* translates something like "the good seed." That woman has dedicated her life to bringing an end to the good seed renaissance I am trying to generate.

MAUREEN
I still rue the first time I saw that weed of yours appearing suddenly in our lake …

ARTHUR
You "rue" that, huh? And wild rice is not a weed …

MAUREEN
A rose by any other name, Mr. Copper.

ARTHUR
You can't eat roses, lady. You know the type: upper-middle-class. Husband was some bigwig though it's obvious she wears the Bermuda shorts in that family. Works in the upper offices of some big hospital. A perpetual glass of white wine in her hand and listens continuously to CBC Radio to expand her world outlook. Her cottage property ends right at the shoreline, but you get the impression she thinks she owns the whole lake. Or at the very least, has taken responsibility for the lake. I respect strong women. Been surrounded by them most of my life … my mother, my wife, my daughter. But this woman …

MAUREEN

Yes?

ARHTUR

Nothing. Nothing. Let me just say, there's a lot of me and
my family up there and all over this lake. You could say we
are this lake.

MAUREEN

Oh please, you are not this lake. Your family is not "this
lake." We are all this lake.

ARTHUR

What are you, a socialist or something? NDP?

MAUREEN

Oh God no. We are all Canadians I mean. I don't know
why you have such trouble accepting that. I love this lake
as much as you do.

ARTHUR

Oh yeah? Without this lake, there'd be no Arthur Copper,
and I'd like to think that without Arthur Copper and
my family, this lake wouldn't be the same either. You
see, my father was actually born here. Up there, beside
that drumlin. You see, that area used to be our traditional
trapping grounds. A hundred or a thousand years
or so ago, just before Time Immemorial became the
twentieth century. My grandfather and his father, all these
generations of our family, used to trap up there – all the
way down to the lake. Martin, beaver, mink, muskrat. If it

had fur, we would trap it. It was what we did. It was who we were, living in unison with the land. I grew up hearing stories of those days. Great stories. Hard-to-believe stories. Our stories.

For instance, Carl Benojee, my grandfather's cousin once-removed from his wife's sister, broke his leg up there. Had to crawl all the way down that tree-covered hill, then across this frozen lake to get help. Young people don't do that today. This expanse of water is already not the same. My grandfather and great-grandfather wouldn't recognize it. I barely do. This one here, it's battling for its identity. Its existence.

MAUREEN
Me thinks thou doth protest too much.

ARTHUR
You think that, doth thou?

MAUREEN
Indeed I do. Yes the area has become somewhat suburbanized, but that is not necessarily a bad thing.

ARTHUR
Yes there are two Tim Hortons now. I can't argue with that.

MAUREEN
Oh don't underestimate yourself. I'm sure you'd find a way. Or are you saying we finally found something about non-Native culture you don't want to complain about?

**ARTHUR**

*Jiindan Ndanishnaabenbag diyaash.*

**MAUREEN**

Oh, some pithy words of Aboriginal wisdom?

**ARTHUR**

It means, "Kiss my flat Indian ass."

*ARTHUR steps out of the canoe onto the stage.*

What? You thought I was out on the lake? Silly people.
You don't have to be on the water to sit in a canoe,
anymore then you have to be on a highway to sit in a car.
A canoe can just be a nice place to think. To ponder the
world. So much intelligence, trial and error, and history
is in a good handmade canoe, it can't help but focus
your thoughts. Several years ago, when my wife left us to
follow ... a different path in life ... one that didn't seem
to include me ... one morning just up and gone, just like
that ... I don't know if you have people who do things like
that in your culture ... anyway, I went out canoeing in this
thing. It centred me. Helped me move on. Why need a
wife when you got a canoe? Now this here canoe is older
than me. It's got the wisdom of the ages in its keel, the
knowledge of our ancestors in its ribs. The strength of our
people in its gunwale. The varnish is all Caucasian though.
I think that's why it smells. Over the years a lot of thinking,
fishing, and wild ricing has gone on in this canoe. It has
carried a lot of Native traditions ... and butts over the
last few decades.

I love this canoe, almost as much as I love my daughter Marie. Except this thing will do what I tell it and it's always where I left it. Anyway, you heard me saying things have changed, you don't have to take my word for it. Just look at the lake. (*pointing*) That way and that way, every way, actually. All these lakes around here used to be how my people survived. How we fed our families with fish and animals that drew sustenance from their waters.

Not anymore. Whole different set of rules these days. Over there, and up there. (*pointing*) Cottages. Lots and lots of cottages. All different shapes and sizes. All over the place. If you blink, another one will pop up. And all the things that come with them. Boats, docks, skidoos, flagpoles, Muskoka chairs, hot tubs, fondues, golf courses. God I hate golf courses. An acre uses up more water than a square mile of forest. Now don't get me wrong, I kinda like the idea of taking a big stick and whacking a couple of small white balls …

MAUREEN
Have you ever played golf?

ARTHUR
Do I look like I play golf?

MAUREEN
I happen to know for a fact many Native people play golf. Quite a few, in fact. So I find your argument problematic if not contrary.

ARTHUR

Yeah? Well, I happen to know a lot of non-Natives that happen to like *manoomin* and what I'm doing here. Non-Natives ... is that the right word? I keep losing track of the politically correct term for them: "non-Native," "settler," "people of pallor," "colour-challenged," "pigment-denied" ... I don't know. We call them *Chugnash*. Not that I have anything against them mind you ... some of my best friends are white. Or whitish ... cream ... snow ... ivory ...

MAUREEN

I don't suppose your reserve has an HR department? That sounds suspiciously like racism.

ARTHUR

Oh does it? I am not a racist. I'm Anishnawbe.

MAUREEN

Anish ... nobby ... What exactly does that word mean?

ARTHUR

Well, if you must know, it means the first or original people.

MAUREEN

First or original people ... and that doesn't sound just a tad ... selective or elitist?

ARTHUR

No ...

MAUREEN

Welcome to the twenty-first century, Mr. Copper,
everybody can be racist. And yes, I may be so-called white,
but people from many different lands and cultures have
cottages all across this country. Did you forget that?

ARTHUR

Yes I know there are lots of other people from lots of other
countries around the world inhabiting this land, but most
of them don't seem to have this same bizarre need for
driving hundreds of kilometres away from their home in
a city, bordering on a huge lake, to spend time and money
on another home, bordering on a smaller lake.

> *MAUREEN begins to take the
> chicken off the barbeque.*

MAUREEN

What Mr. Copper doesn't know is that for many years
I practiced Buddhism, which as you may know, is quite
anti-racist. Still, it has been a bit of a journey for me.
When I was growing up in Sudbury back in the ... well,
let's just say it was a few years ago. I'd see Native people
here and there. Yes they were in the schools and on the
streets and everywhere. But I never really got to know
any of them, beyond a cursory hello or occasional social
function. I have even been to a powwow once, back in the
late eighties. That was before people began claiming I was
"anti-Indigenous." That is so silly. I have nothing against
them. My father did though. Once told me not to get too
friendly with them. Native people had a reputation for

drinking too much he would say, completely forgetting the fact we were half-Irish and he was no stranger to a wide assortment of cocktails himself. Said they were lazy and didn't want to work, and yet it was mostly my mother and her job that paid most of the bills.

ARTHUR

I bet you grew up watching the Lone Ranger and Tonto. "What we do now, Kemosabe?"

MAUREEN

Actually, that was a little before me. I grew up watching *The Beachcombers*. And oddly, I don't remember Jesse Jim planting any wild rice just off Gibsons' shores.

ARTHUR

Well ... that was on the ocean ... and ... *manoomin* doesn't grow ...

MAUREEN

Again you miss the point, but I digress. We bought this cottage five years after we got married. It seems the fifth wedding anniversary is wood. So voila, a pine cottage surrounded by willow and poplar trees. I cried. We'd had a rough year, my young Cameron again with a heart murmur, and after we had it treated, Justin bought this for us. I think to congratulate us both for persevering. That summer, believe it or not, Justin learned to water-ski. Till he dislocated his knee. He always tried to be the real he-man type. Six foot one, a trim one hundred ninety. He loved this lake and cottage, but unfortunately they seemed they didn't love him back quite as much. Still, all he had to do was sit on his deck chair, look out on this view, and it made him happy.

Now at the time we knew there was a Native community in the vicinity. I mean, for the amount of money we were putting down, we investigated the whole area. There's a nice provincial park just a few kilometres north of here and the hospital is easily within a half hour's drive. This Otter Lake seemed like a nice reserve ... sorry, First Nation. It seemed like a nice First Nation. Not like some of those tragic places you see on the news.

We even went on a field trip there way back when. A lovely village for sure. And bonus, we discovered the gas is a lot cheaper there. My husband was an accountant with one of the larger firms and he appreciated that. But of course the half-hour drive there and back sort of mitigated the financial benefits of the discount, so it didn't make sense to take advantage of it. But on the bright side, we did pick up some lovely beaded slippers.

We ... I have been there only once since then, for obvious reasons. You see, now I'm known as the crazy, racist, anti-Indigenous woman. Truth be told, I think that's completely unfair. Evil people don't have RRSPs, dammit.

ARTHUR
Sure they do.

MAUREEN
Oh. Do you? Have any RRSPs I mean?

ARTHUR
Me? Yeah but we call it a Reserve Reconciliation Savings
Plan. (*walking to the shoreline*) You want to see evil ... here,
I want to show you something evil.

> *ARTHUR reaches into the water and*
> *pulls out some long grasslike plants.*

All of this beautiful *manoomin*, dead. I have spent hours
telling my daughter about what is in my hand, because
on this slender and delicate stalk hangs a sizable sad and
tragic story. I plant, grow, and harvest *manoomin* in the age
of Twitter and Keurig coffee. And that simple fact pisses
a lot of these here people off. I'm not pointing fingers
or anything ...

> *Instead he points a lip in MAUREEN's*
> *direction. She rolls her eyes.*

ARTHUR
As placid as this lake may look, there is a war, however
benign, waging along its calm, manicured shores.
　　But first, you need context, a history lesson. In 1497 a
man named John Cabot started things off when, as was
the custom back then, he was on his way to China and
somehow hit North America. I can understand this, I was
once on my way to Newmarket and somehow ended up
in Brampton. These things happen. Several hundred years
passed and before you know it, the gradual colonization of
Canada was well on its way.

Around here, this was prime hunting and agricultural land. Our rivers and lakes were our highways and fields. There were Nish scattered all around, wandering and wondering when the first KFC would open. But before there was anyone, there was *manoomin*. You know how in the Bible it says, "In the beginning was the word?" Well in our culture, in the beginning was *manoomin*. And it was good.

MAUREEN
Oh now you're making fun of the Bible?! You're comparing the word of God with a water plant?!

ARTHUR
Does that offend you?

MAUREEN
It would offend any Christian.

ARTHUR
I thought you said you were a Buddhist?

MAUREEN
I was, and I think it's possible to walk both paths.

ARTHUR
You sure?! I'm having difficulty trying to imagine a Buddhist residential school.

MAUREEN

Aha! I knew you'd bring up residential schools. I just knew it. For your information, sir, I and everybody I know had nothing to do with those.

ARTHUR

That sounds pretty impassioned. Are you trying to convince me or yourself?

MAUREEN

Neither. Just setting the record straight. (*pause*) Okay, try and follow how stupid this story is. It all began innocently enough. My husband and I were puttering around the backyard, you know, doing cottagey things. I was putting my tulip bulbs in, hopefully in such a way those damn squirrels wouldn't get them. Again. Justin was cleaning the gutters of the first leaf fall of the season. He was leaning rather heavily on the ladder, looking unusually tired. I was just about to comment when we heard it. It was hard not to hear. Sounded like a small plane taking off, or a really big Sea-Doo. We didn't know what it was. What it was ... was Mr. Arthur Copper and that infernal machine of his. That's when it began.

ARTHUR

You're talking about *Gertie*. She's talking about *Gertie*. Don't you go slandering my girl. *Gertie's* my baby.

MAUREEN

Your so called "*Gertie*" is not a girl. And definitely not a baby. I don't know what it is except maybe a mechanical monster. It was the beginning. For most of my adult life I worked in a hospital in Scarborough. Human Resources. I thought I'd seen just about every kind of conflict you could think imaginable. But seriously, being a point guard in a battle with Native people over something as innocuous as wild rice?!?! How much more Canadian can you get then that?

ARTHUR

I'd actually been planting *manoomin* for several years already, in various other lakes with just my daughter to help me, and I'd only just got to this one. By then, I had it down to a science.

MAUREEN

I am not a bad person. But neither is Arthur Copper a saint. His is not a holy crusade as he implies. His is an arrogant attempt at using his heritage to hijack this lake and all the other lakes around here. Somehow I became the focal point of this insane disagreement, all because I wanted to preserve the cottage, shoreline, and lake the way we bought it. The way we remember it. Cameron, my oldest, learned to walk right there. Caught his first fish over there. According to family rumour, kissed his first girl in our hot tub. That was before he had that minor falling out with his father. Over that Kickstarter fraud incident. (*pause*) He was young. And my precious Terri-Lynn, she learned to swim off the tip of this dock. So determined and confident. Justin had to drag her out of this very lake at least three times before she nearly drowned. But by God, she learned. In grade eleven she represented her school in one of those provincial swimming competitions. Came in second. Thanks to this lake. I am not sure if there is a connection but she's working on her master's in kinesiology in Florida. I still remember her jumping off this dock. Was that only yesterday ... of course, that was pre–wild rice infestation. Doubt she could swim much out there now.

ARTHUR

I protest your use of the word "infestation."

MAUREEN

That's all you do, protest. It's people like you that give Native people a bad name.

ARTHUR

I do? No I don't.

MAUREEN

Oh yes, you most certainly do.

ARTHUR

Prove it.

MAUREEN

Okay. If you wish, I could give you a long, detailed list. Annotated, complete with references and footnotes, including a comprehensive etymology.

ARTHUR

(*using a thick Indian accent*) I do not understand this
language you call English. It says things but then does not
say things. It is very confusing. (*switching back to normal*)
Now to understand the true story of what's happening on
these lakes, you need some traditional teachings. Normally
you would give me some *sammon* for these teachings ...

MAUREEN

Salmon?

ARTHUR

Not salmon. *Sammon. Sammon.* Tobacco. As a way of
asking for teachings or giving thanks.

MAUREEN

You thank people by giving them ... tobacco? That's
so bizarre.

ARTHUR

Right, this coming from people who drink the blood of
their Saviour. I think of it as a sliding scale. Be that as it
may, I will share this teaching ... pro bono. These lakes ...
all these lakes ... they're fields of food for all the Creator's
creatures, both above and below the waterline. They are
highways that have taken my people and yours all across
this country. They provide water to drink and cook in.
To bathe in. A lake is so much more than a place to put
your cottage. But some people don't see that.

You could hear the *manoomin* beckoning to the people
on shore, "Come harvest me. Let me feed your people.

We have thirty percent of your daily protein needs. Forty-four percent of your magnesium requirements, not to mention a whole bunch of good iron and potassium to help wrestle those moose." And don't get me started on the fibre, man. You heard me say how shitty things are now. That's why you need good fibre. Next to a bowl of sawdust, nothing beats *manoomin*.

Know what makes an Anishnawbe an Anishnawbe? See if their breath smells of *manoomin*. Won't be long before somebody makes a friggin' cologne out of it. So imagine it. This is the way it has been since Time Immemorial. Before Canada. Before the voyageurs. Before everything. Come the late fall, as predictable as the birds flying south for the winter, a slender, purposeful canoe enters the cool water of this lake, following a course that is practically ingrained in its wooden fibres. In that same canoe are two people.

*Getting back in the canoe, ARTHUR*
*demonstrates his actions.*

One in the front paddling and steering, another at the back, with two two-foot-long sticks. This person uses one stick to bend a handful of the *manoomin* stalks over into the boat, and uses the other stick to gently whack the tip of the plant, knocking the wild rice itself into the bottom of the boat. Just back and forth along the shore, paddling and harvesting until you fill up your canoe, leaving a nice respectable amount floating on the water, floating for the moment, then sinking through the water to the mud beneath, ready to take root for next year's harvest. Marie, my daughter, was a natural. It's almost a ballet the way she did it. Then after getting back to shore, we'd dry it, dance on it. Oh she would dance up a storm on that *manoomin*. That's how you separate the chafe from the grain. When you've got boatloads of the stuff, I've got a mechanical machine that can do that pretty quickly, but I still have a soft spot in my heart for doing it by foot.

*He demonstrates the rice dancing.*

When I would see Marie dancing her heart out on that blanket, I could see my grandmother, and her grandmother, and her grandmother. All I could see were grandmothers preparing *manoomin* for their children. And for a brief second, I saw my daughter as a future grandmother. And it felt good. Then you roast *manoomin* on a fire, or in a roaster. And then you eat it. That has been the pattern for more generations then anybody can remember. For us, it's a form of food sovereignty.

MAUREEN
And just how does your daughter feel about your hijinks out here on the lake? And in the newspapers? And on television? A little embarrassed perhaps?

ARTHUR
You don't know my Marie. She's always one for fighting a good fight. She believes in what I'm doing.

MAUREEN
Why isn't she here now? With you?

*ARTHUR is silent for a moment.*

ARTHUR
She is. She's here, but not here.

MAUREEN
Again, he evades the question. Okay. I can understand a
lot of what Mr. Copper is attempting to do. Yes I am sure
they have lost many of their traditions. Yes in many cases
white people have been responsible. But what the hell
does that have to do with this lake? And if you can believe
it, I actually like wild rice! Seriously I do. My brother's
wife makes a simply lovely chicken soup with it. She's got
this gluten-free thing and supposedly its better than barley
in the soup. So there. I watched *Dances with Wolves*. As I
mentioned, I've been to a powwow. I've got a Benjamin
Chee Chee on my wall. Dreamcatchers ... three. I've read
Tom King and Joseph Boyden.

ARTHUR
I think that last one qualifies as a hit ... and a miss.

MAUREEN
So I have no problem with Native people. But he
provokes us! Seriously, he does. That horrible
machine of Mr. Copper's I mentioned earlier?!?!

> *The sound of* Gertie *can be heard
> in the background, gradually getting
> louder and louder, till it's almost
> impossible to hear MAUREEN.*

It looks like something out of a "Mad Max Tours the Florida Everglades" movie. It's got this big propeller on the back and it sort of just skips across the water. Incredibly noisy. And our lake is normally so calm. When we saw him that fall afternoon, just tearing across the water, scaring the ducks and loons, we had no idea who it was or what he was doing. We just thought, "How rude!" and ... (*suddenly screaming*) WILL YOU SHUT OFF YOUR STUPID ENGINE?!

> *The noise disappears.*
> *MAUREEN tries to refocus herself.*

ARTHUR
What did you just call me?

MAUREEN
What? No! I said engine! Engine!

ARTHUR
Sure you did.

MAUREEN
As I was saying, I have no idea what that loud contraption has to do with Native culture, which supposedly is what this whole disagreement is about. The right to reinstate their Indigenous ways is how I believe he puts it. It seems he was planting seeds. Wild rice seeds. But does he have to reinstate it ten feet from my dock?! In that thing? And I was unaware that Native people had invented the four-stroke internal combustion machine. I mean, really, it doesn't even look like a canoe. Or a kayak.

ARTHUR

With that kind of logic, does my truck have to look like a horse for me to get around? Do my steel-toed work boots have to be made from moosehide? Times change and so do Native people.

MAUREEN

But you're the one who talks incessantly about the need to preserve your traditions. At our expense. So I can't help but notice just how selective you're being about what is convenient for your needs and inconvenient for ours. I don't suppose you notice a contradiction there?! Huh? Well?

ARTHUR

So if I was to do this all by canoe alone, that would be okay?

MAUREEN

Of course not. It would still be the same issue.

ARTHUR

Just a quieter issue?! Traditionally we used to harvest, with canoes and sticks, fine to do when you have the time or are just showing people how things are done. But it's kind of hard to make a serious dent in your mortgage doing it that way ... if I had a mortgage. I mean, we move on, as individuals and as people. We are Aboriginals of the twenty-first century. We used to hunt deer and moose with a bow and arrow or a spear. We use these things now called guns. The simple fact that I'm using a gas-powered mechanical device that utilizes concepts invented over the last two hundred years by your people infuriates some of these persons. Their logic being, if we want to eat traditionally, we have to gather it traditionally, or what they believe "traditionally" is. So I guess we can only eat baloney that we run off a cliff.

So keeping in that spirit, I got me something just a little more powerful than a canoe. It's a bigger boat, kinda pretty in its own ugly way. Except ... it's gotta motor. A kick-ass motor! It puts those fucking Sea-Doos to shame! With it, I can harvest an entire lake like this in maybe two or three days. In a single canoe, couple weeks. A fleet of canoes, maybe seven or nine days. Keeping in mind, of course, *manoomin* can ripen at different times. So all that product on a couple of litres of gas. It's a beautiful machine, practically put it together myself. Big fan on the backside, seat in the middle for steering, and up front, huge broad shovel specially designed for the scooping up of *manoomin*. I don't know what you're getting so upset about. It's economical and efficient. Don't you settler types get off on that kind of thing? So how's that chicken coming along?

*MAUREEN holds up her barbeque fork to ARTHUR.*

MAUREEN
See this?

*ARTHUR nods.*

MAUREEN

Fork ... you. Now leaving that monstrosity aside, over
the winter, much like this controversy, those horrid seeds
he planted ... lay there in the mud, growing, getting
stronger, about to spring forth upon the world. The calm
before the storm.

ARTHUR

Time for another history lesson: you see, times changed,
the lake changed, and the people who spent time on these
shores changed. These different people built canals and
locks that played around with the water levels. The bottom
would be dug up, then log booms would churn everything
up. The water became poisoned with new and unfriendly
things. Strange new plants from faraway places suddenly
began choking the life from the *manoomin*. It almost went
away, just like Native people. What a coinkydink huh?

And then these new people who started crowding
the water ways and shores, they had a different view
of this plant. Unimportant. A nuisance. For some odd
reason, they wanted to get what they called "rice" from
some faraway places. As with all things that are unloved
and neglected, the *manoomin* began to die off. To some,
it became just a memory. But the Anishnawbe, we have
very strong memories.

. This is one of the things I would teach my daughter.
One beautiful summer day, I took her out on a lake, the
*manoomin* was just beginning to stick up through the
water, reaching for the sun. I talked to her about how
*manoomin* is more than just a plant. How we are more
than just humans. People like the demon in khakis over

there don't understand that. We are related. Interrelated actually, in so many complex manners, that whole web/ Gaia theory ... yeah, I watch documentaries. First of all, you need shallow, clean water, which is good for everyone. Good rich soil. Lots of sunlight. But then who doesn't need those? You should see when I harvest bags of the stuff. Lots of bugs and insects crawling all through it. All different kinds. An insect doctor's wet dream. You see, these insects live off the plants, and those that don't live off the insects that do. Add to that all the birds, frogs, snakes, and other animals that consider a *manoomin* field a food court because of those insects. Then you got the next level in the predatory hierarchy ... you vegetarians might not want to listen to this, um ... contemplate a carrot for a second. You see, next you have the fish, birds, otters, etcetera, who then feed on those smaller creatures. And so on up the food chain. So you see, when a *manoomin* field dies, more than a few straggly plants are the casualties. It's an entire biosphere. My daughter ... she understood.

MAUREEN

Could it possibly be that you're over-complicating things? Romanticizing the situation perhaps?

ARTHUR

What can I say, I'm a romantic.

MAUREEN

I wish I could say Mr. Copper was the only battle I had that season. That winter we got the diagnosis for Justin. The doctors said there were several treatment options.

"There's always hope," they said. Sometimes during the winter we'd come up to the cottage. A week at Christmas, maybe Easter, or on occasion, just for the hell of it. It's so quiet during winter. It's almost as if the snow is a big sound blanket. But that winter, for obvious reasons, we never made it up. (*pause*) Spring. My husband was doing well ... not great but well. We come out to the cottage earlier than normal. We've both got leave from our jobs and he needs time and peace to recover from the treatments. It wasn't for a couple weeks or so till I began to notice it. It's like the lake was developing a five o'clock shadow. I knew this lake like the back of my hand but something different was happening. At first I thought it might be seaweed of some sort. Occasionally we would have something called milfoil clog up the shoreline. Horrible stuff. Makes everything look like a swamp. But this didn't look like milfoil. We didn't know what it was. But it was growing.

It was Greg McBoyd, my next-door neighbour ... in a lovely A-frame with a stone patio and built-in hot tub, who told me it was wild rice. He'd heard a rumour that some Native guy had been planting it all up and down the lake. And in a few other lakes too.

ARTHUR
Me! That was me! In case you weren't sure ...

*MAUREEN takes a deep breath and carries on.*

MAUREEN

"Can he do this?" I asked Greg. He shrugged. That's his response to ninety percent of any questions asked him. We had a couple of friends over to visit Justin, and they were all talking about this guy named Arthur Copper, who had decided to repopulate the lakes with this Wild Rice. It was him we saw last fall in that big machine. I mean, in principal, we support Native issues, but to do this, without consulting us … again, how rude.

After a few phone calls, we found out this wild rice was popping up in a dozen different lakes all over the area, thanks to Mr. Copper. These gorgeous, beautiful lakes we all love and adore were now beginning to look like marshes. This was not right. This affected property values, resale issues, water-safety concerns. So logic dictated I chat with Mr. Copper myself. I just hoped Mr. Copper was a reasonable man.

*This becomes a conversation: ARTHUR is trying to eat his cereal. MAUREEN is out on the dock with a big mug of tea.*

ARTHUR

My phone rings. I pick it up. "*Aaniin,*" I say.

MAUREEN

Did he just call me "honey"? Ah yes. Is this Mr. Copper? Arthur Copper?

ARTHUR
It be I.

MAUREEN
Mr. Copper. My name is Maureen Poole and I have a
cottage on Starling Lake.

ARTHUR
Well, good for you.

MAUREEN
Uh this is kind of awkward. I understand you are the
gentleman responsible for this recent growth of plant
material in the lake system.

ARTHUR
Again, that would be I. Would you like to buy some
when it ripens?

MAUREEN
No I most certainly would not. In fact, I am phoning
to complain.

ARTHUR
Is this just a general complaint or do you have something
specific you'd like to complain about?

MAUREEN
I understand you have been planting wild rice seeds all
over the local lakes. It and you are responsible for ruining
many of the waterways. What do you plan to do about it?

ARTHUR

Lady, it's almost eleven o'clock on a Sunday morning. Not
my best time for pop quizzes. What would you like me to
do about it?

MAUREEN

Well, if you must know, I would like you to stop spreading
your seed where it's not wanted.

ARTHUR

I hope you're talking about *manoomin*.

MAUREEN

Of course I am. The point is your *man ... mano ...* wild
rice is bringing down our property values. Those
lakes belong to all of us. Not just you. You don't even
live near us.

ARTHUR

I am going to take a shot in the dark and say neither do
you. I bet you live in or about Toronto most of the time.
Yeah I live two lakes over but I think my connection with
that lake is a lot stronger historically than anything you
could come up with. By the way, my cereal is getting soggy
and I'm missing *Coronation Street*.

MAUREEN

I was hoping to reason with you, Mr. Copper. Several of
us cottage owners disagree with your perspective. If you
do not desist, we will take you to court. There are safety
violations involved, those weeds you planted can damage

boats and endanger swimmers. Are you prepared to deal
with being sued, Mr. Copper?

ARTHUR

You ... you want to sue me? For planting *manoomin*?
Well, let me describe my *manoomin* empire that you are
so eager to possess. I have a twenty-year-old television
that gets more snow than Iqaluit. A couch that is older
than my daughter. A stove with two broken elements.
A roof that on rainy days doubles as my shower. All
enclosed in what could be called an antique trailer. *Ambe
Chaganash zhii kwe.*

MAUREEN

And just what does that mean?

ARTHUR

"Bring it on, white lady."

MAUREEN

He hung up on me. This is not how I expected to
spend my later years, doing battle with an Aboriginal
horticulturalist gone mad. While my husband was lying
there sick. I had two glasses of wine that afternoon.

ARTHUR

If you need one, I know an alcohol counsellor. She can
help you get that Chardonnay monkey off your back.

MAUREEN

I suppose you don't drink, Mr. Copper?

ARTHUR

On occasion I've been known to enjoy a glass of wine. But much like my dating preferences, I prefer mine warm and red, not cold and white.

MAUREEN

Turns out there was very little we could do legally. Our property rights go down to the shoreline but ends there. The province, or more specifically the Ministry of Natural Resources, owns everything past that. So, we were stymied. Just another tragic example of the Cottager's Burden. Every day that hideous plant seemed to grow a good inch at least. So, we ... meaning me ... had threatened some action.

So Greg McBoyd and Mark Albany came up with an interesting idea. Personally, I hated that it had come to this but Justin was getting weaker and I wanted his recuperation to be spent looking out at the lake we had first glimpse so many years ago. So while I took my husband to one of his appointments at the hospital, Greg and Mark did their thing. It felt rather clandestine, but we had no choice.

ARTHUR

Sure you did.

MAUREEN

No we did not. That stuff was growing. Every day was becoming increasingly hazardous.

ARTHUR

This is when the disagreement became a war.

MAUREEN

As always, you exaggerate.

ARTHUR

Tell them what you did, then.

MAUREEN

I didn't do it. (*pause*) You see, Jim and Mark ... well ...
they each had a Sea-Doo ...

ARTHUR

And?

MAUREEN

And ... well ... a thin piece of rope.

ARTHUR

I had almost forgotten about my little conversation with
the devil-in-flip-flops. A couple weeks passed and harvest
season was fast approaching. As best as I can remember,
it was a Tuesday morning. About ten. Sun was high and
inviting, beaming down as if to say, "Winter's coming,
better get that *manoomin* in before that northern wind
starts blowing." A forty-minute ride from my house to
where I launch my boat into the water.

About half a dozen metres offshore, I saw a mess of
something green floating on top of the water. About three
or four metres across. It took me a second before I realized

what it was. I saw all my beautiful *manoomin* plants laying
there, dead. I couldn't figure out what had happened.
A storm wouldn't do that. *Manoomin* plants are tough.
Strong. Resilient. Something unnatural and destructive
had reeked its vengeance down upon these innocent
plants. There could only be one answer. Botanical
genocide. That's what it was … it was the Fifth Horseman
of the Apocalypse. Cottagers!

MAUREEN

We couldn't swim, we couldn't fish. Desperate people do
desperate things.

ARTHUR

Fifty years ago there were businesses all up and down this
lake where my father wasn't allowed to enter. Maybe he
should have decapitated all of them.

MAUREEN

Again, I had no control of what happened back then.
I wasn't happy about what we'd done. And of course
in its own way, our little plan backfired. Those two had
managed to kill off a good number of those plants but of
course they were still there. Floating on the water. Dead,
but not going anywhere. Most of it just floated there, as if
taunting us. Meanwhile, Justin was getting weaker. He was
putting up a valiant fight but nobody really expected him
to survive past the summer. Everybody was giving me
that false sense of hope. "Justin is a fighter. If anybody can
pull through it will be him." Carl from across the bay told
me, "Don't count Justin out. He might just surprise all of

us." But he wouldn't. I knew. The doctors, though vainly struggling to be positive, knew. And Justin knew. He now spent most of his days wrapped in a blanket, on our back patio, watching the world pass by on our lake. It helped. He watched the ice on it melt that spring, saw storms come and go, even saw an island of cattails detach and float across the bay. A lot would happen out there on the water but the lake itself never changed. Everything else did. Everything good in our family has happened out here in this cottage, on this lake.

Terri-Lynn kept flying up from Florida. It was so expensive and she came dangerously close to losing her university year for missing so much. I had to put my foot down and tell her this wasn't really accomplishing much. Her father knew she loved him, and throwing her year away was not in anybody's best interest. And Cameron … well, being the baby of the family we always had to be strong for him. Hold his hand during the rougher times. For all his flaws, Cameron was there for his father in the end.

Justin and I were planning to retire here someday. He was actually a transplanted American, you know, who had long ago adopted the belief that Canada had more opportunities for him. He always said, he'd been born an American but would die a Canadian.

By now Justin was so weak and drugged even the sounds of hell couldn't wake him. I had just put my husband down for a nap when I heard that machine of his. Out in the middle of the lake. He stopped at one of the floating islands of dead plants. I saw him sprinkle something on them.

ARTHUR

*Sammon.*

MAUREEN

Again with the tobacco. You do know that's bad for you.

ARTHUR

Just the way white people prepare it.

MAUREEN

And just why do you feel the need to spread your tobacco on the water?

ARTHUR

I felt sorry for my *manoomin,* now dead. It was my way of honouring it.

MAUREEN

I don't understand.

ARTHUR

Yeah, I know. You see, it's all part of the great web of Aboriginal tradition. Speaking of which (*turning to the audience*): We acknowledge that we walk upon the Traditional Territories of the Mississaugas of the New Credit First Nation, Anishnawbe, Haudenosaunee, and Wendat Indigenous Peoples, the original nations of this land, who continue to cry out for justice.

MAUREEN

Was that really necessary?

ARTHUR
I'm sorry. Did you want to do it?


MAUREEN
A lot of people cry out for justice. Justice can have many
names and many faces. It became the summer of our
mutual discontent.


ARTHUR
As you might expect, things got worse. As the plants
grew taller and stronger, I would find more and more
*manoomin* pulled up or sliced under. People along the lake
would stop talking to me, which is odd considering I'm
such a nice, adorable guy. Once I found a bunch of dead
*manoomin*, about a foot and a half deep, dumped at the
front of my driveway. When I was out in the canoe, I'd
get the finger. One cottager, when he did this, I tried to
explain to him that in Anishnawbe culture, that's a sign
of blessing, of sexual vitality. It's not really, but it sure
confused the hell out of him. We do that all the time to
white people ... oh don't tell anyone.


MAUREEN
And you wonder why people don't like you ...


ARTHUR
Another time, there was a whole field of *manoomin* at the
other end of the lake that was dead, but I couldn't figure
out why. They hadn't been cut. There was a couple of dead
fish too. Something was deadly wrong. Curious, I tasted
the water. Salty. Very salty. Somebody had dumped

a block of salt in the middle of these plants. It would gradually erode, and the shift in pH had killed them. And a few other things ...

MAUREEN

I did not approve of that. I don't care what you think, but seriously, that was not me. I thought the idea was stupid. I mean, wouldn't that poison the very lake we were trying to save? Greg swore up and down the size of the lake and the current would dissipate the salt and only the wild rice in the immediate area would receive a full dosage.

ARTHUR

Of course, the angrier I got, the more seeds I planted. I would let the *manoomin* talk for me. My vengeance would be a lush and healthy lake. With that bullet in my gun, I could not go wrong. Or so I thought. I found out the hard way, you take the "t" out of "Native," you get "naive."

MAUREEN

Admittedly, things were getting a bit out of hand.

ARTHUR

Did you say you admit it?!

MAUREEN

Sorry, I can't hear you. My hearing seems to have been damaged by a whole summer of loud, ear-splitting, mechanical thunder.

ARTHUR

That's okay, you're not the first settler who for some reason can't hear the voices of Canada's Indigenous population.

MAUREEN

I hate that term. Settlers. My father's family have been here since the mid-1800s. My mother's, a generation before that. We are not settlers. We are Canadians in every sense of the word.

ARTHUR

Sorry, having trouble making out what you're saying over the background hum of white privilege.

MAUREEN

Again with the race card.

*Beat.*

Salvation can come in many forms. In this particular case it was called a dredger. Big huge thing that looks like it shouldn't be able to float. What it does is grab the seaweed, pull it up and spit it into a wide bin located on its back. We managed to convince the province to send one of theirs. I am nothing if not convincing when I have to be. I mean, I am in HR. Besides, that was our tax money at work. You'd never think you'd need a dredger until you needed one I guess. Normally I am rather critical of the many unneeded and unnecessary programs the province feels the need to invest in, but in this instance, I thought "Why wasn't there a second? And a third dredger?"

Our will was strong, but we were just humble cottagers, unversed in the ways of rural warfare. We needed bigger guns. And luckily, the province had such big guns. A week later, there it was, cruising into our end of the lake. I never thought such an ugly thing would be so beautiful. Pretty soon our lake would be free of wild rice, and our boating and swimming habits would return to pre–Arthur Copper days.

*ARTHUR is out in* Gertie.

ARTHUR
I was out taking inventory of what was ripening where, when I saw something lumbering through the water. Making its way slowly across the once-placid lake was a huge, hulking, mechanical behemoth of some sort. There was literally a tank out on the water. Evidently somebody had gone deep into the arcane archives of the Ministry of Natural Resources and found out you can get a permit to yank harmful lake weeds. Gee, I wonder who that was?

MAUREEN
(*raising her glass*) *Salut.*

ARTHUR
This big beast was making its way across the lake, chewing up fields of wild rice and spitting it out like they were nothing more than sunflower seed shells. I immediately thought two things: what a great metaphor for Canada's treatment of its Native people. And second … I was now pissed. I was angry. I was going into warrior mode. That

thing was scarring up my lake. It was eating my *manoomin*.
So I revved up my airboat and went tank hunting.

Directly ahead of it, about half a kilometre, was a lush
stand of wild rice. It waved beautifully in the summer
air, beckoning, unaware of the rapidly approaching death
machine. I opened the throttle on *Gertie*, as full as she'd go.
I was going warp eight at least. I now know how perilous
it is when Scottie goes, "She canna' hold it, Captain. She'll
fly apart!" It seemed the only thing holding *Gertie* together
was my belief in what we were doing.

*MAUREEN is comfortable in a Muskoka chair.*

MAUREEN

A few of us were on my dock, watching that machine do
its thing. Then, we saw Mr. Copper's ... boat ... suddenly
appear at the other end of the lake. Immediately I
thought ... "He wouldn't ... He's not that crazy ...
Is he?" Are you?

ARTHUR

Ask my ex-wife. It was a race. Salvation vs. destruction.
Food vs. landfill. Culture vs. cultural ignorance. *Gertie*
was fueled by fifty percent gas and fifty percent righteous
cause. I flew across the water. Dragon flies and gnats
whizzed by us in an blur, I could almost hear them
encouraging me above *Gertie's* mighty roar. Though we
were going all out, it almost seemed like we were crawling.
That monstrosity, despite its size, was closing at a good
clip. But *Gertie*, sensing my outrage, somehow managed

to find a little extra, somewhere, somehow. And we went faster. At one point two loons made a panicked dive. These two raccoons on a nearby shore were placing bets ...

MAUREEN
Collectively, our jaws dropped. We had my proof that Arthur Copper was insane. He was playing chicken, or whatever the Aboriginal equivalent is ... duck or chickadee, with a huge mechanical dredger.

ARTHUR
Finally, my heart in my mouth, with the dredger a mere dozen metres away from my *manoomin*, I pulled up in front of it, splashing water a good ten metres. But once I got *Gertie* stabilized, I stood between this technological wall of *manoomin* death and my precious ancestral legacy. The look in the driver's eyes ... well, I actually felt sorry for him. I knew he probably had no idea the desecration he was about to do. He was just a summer student trying to do his seventeen-dollar-an-hour job. And then suddenly, this crazy Anishnawbe comes out of nowhere, in an airboat, almost ramming him. I don't think that's covered in the student dredger's handbook.

MAUREEN
Son of a bitch.

*Beat.*

The dredger stopped!

ARTHUR
*Salut!*

MAUREEN
Both boats just floated there. I'm not sure, but it seemed like they were having a conversation.

ARTHUR
I looked the guy over. Had nice aviator sunglasses ... gets bright out there on the lake. A worn Ministry of Natural Resources baseball cap. Faded jeans with a grey button-up shirt with rolled sleeves. Looked just a few years older than my daughter. The important thing is, he didn't strike me as a guy who would have a cottage. So I said to him, "You can't do this. This is *manoomin*. Wild rice. It has the same right to be in this lake as you or I do."

*ARTHUR becomes the Dredge operator.*

"Yeah well, I don't know anything about that. I have a work order here to remove weeds from this lake. And that's what I'm doing. If you have a problem, call the Ministry. Can you move your boat ... cool airboat, by the way."

MAUREEN
Was he ... are you ... making friends with him?

ARTHUR
I was.

MAUREEN

No … no … that's not allowed.

ARTHUR

It's hard to hate a man with good taste in boats. I am
polite but I refused to move. I have absolutely no wish to
see the inside of a dredger but I was hoping it wouldn't
come to that. Luckily for me his job description does not
include plowing under Native people in airboats. So we
have a stalemate. Sort of an "Oka on Water." But it's almost
quitting time anyway, so he decides to go home, preferring
to see what tomorrow might bring.

MAUREEN

Son of a bitch if the MNR didn't agree with him. Evidently
the Ministry has some sort of agreement or relationship
with First Nations about working together and respecting
each other. Evidently all he needed was some sort of letter
of support from his community, and he could do whatever
he wanted out there.

ARTHUR

Yay! Government comes to the rescue of an Indigenous
man and his Indigenous culture. There's a sentence I
thought I'd never say.

MAUREEN

You guys just have the governments wrapped around your
fingers, don't you?

ARTHUR

Are you talking to me?!


MAUREEN

It seems that man has a right to plant those plants in the
lake as long as he has a letter of support from his reserve ...
I mean First Nation. As my son would say, "That sucks."
But who respects us cottagers? Do you know how much
money we pump into the local economy?!?! The small
towns around here rely on us. No, pity the poor Indians ...
I mean First Nations ... Aboriginal ... First Nation ...
Indigenous ... whatever the current term is. This is when
the HR in me kicked in. Maybe I am being a bit biased ...
dare I say ... discriminatory? All things are possible.
Could it be?

*Animatedly, ARTHUR puts his hand up.*


ARTHUR

I know! I know! Can I answer?!


MAUREEN

(*to ARTHUR*) No. (*to audience*) It occurred to me that I
am blaming all Native people for the actions of just one
man. I mean really, how many non-Native people have
done stupid and disrespectful things and not had their
entire race condemned. So in the interest of cross-cultural
good relations, I decided to go further up the food chain.
Arthur Copper comes from a First Nation community.
They have leaders ... Chiefs. All leaders are politicians and
politicians know which battles to fight. But first ...

*MAUREEN is silent. She takes a sip of*
*her wine, and looks back at the cottage.*

MAUREEN
I had something that needed doing. My husband ...
well he ... passed away ... just after the dredger incident.
Quietly. In his sleep, in the local hospital. Two days
before, he had lapsed into a coma. It was like he just let
go. For a year he had fought a good battle. Our children
returned one last time to see their father. There were tears,
a few laughs. We had a funeral. People came. Not much
more to say.

ARTHUR
There was an article in the paper about her, her husband,
and this whole issue. That's when I saw the person behind
the glass of white wine. I debated sending a card or flowers,
but thought, maybe I should just stay away. I didn't want
to aggravate her in her moment of grief. I may be a son
of a bitch, but I like to think I was raised properly. That
morning, even though I never met him, I did smudge and
mentioned him in my prayers.

MAUREEN
You did?

ARTHUR
I did.

MAUREEN
I don't know what to say.

*Another moment of silence as* ARTHUR
*picks up the conversation.*

ARTHUR

Maureen Poole went to see our Chief. The man's never
really liked me, ever since I dated his sister back in the late
nineties. That didn't end well. For either of us. I used to
be three inches taller. Being the wily politician, he thinks
we should pick our battles. And compared with Missing
and Murdered Women and Girls, residential schools, teen
suicide, one guy wanting to reintroduce wild rice into our
lakes and riling up the media just is not a battle worth
throwing his weight behind. Mostly it was my relatives on
the council that forced that letter of support out of him,
allowing me to do my thing.

MAUREEN

In the end though, nothing came of the meeting. I can
understand why. A First Nation community voting against
one of its members for doing what he was doing, rightly
or wrongly, would look bad in the light of the media. I'm
on our condo board so I understand. So I went home,
enlightened but not more successful. To the cottage which
suddenly had become so big and empty. And lonely ...
it was a lovely fall afternoon. The kind where the wind
caresses your hair and skin, reminding you that summer
is behind you ... not that far, and winter is just ahead, but
not that close. In all this mess, I hadn't thought what I
would do with the cottage now that ... I was alone. Before,
I had Justin for guidance. Then when he became sick,
I relied on my sense of what was right. Now all I heard was
silence ... in our cottage. On the lake. In my heart.

ARTHUR

I was out on the lake, gathering *manoomin*, in my canoe
this time. *Gertie's* great but every once in a while, you
need time with your canoe. It's a Native thing. The leaves
were just about to change. I had to get as much done as I
could. That's when I saw her cottage. And her standing on
her dock, looking out on this lake. Wearing socks with her
sandals. These people are weird.

MAUREEN

I could see his canoe. And in it, there he sat. Shorter than I
thought. It occurred to me that other than our brief phone
conversation, I had never talked to the man in person.
It took me two seconds before I said those immortal
words that have gotten so many people into trouble. "Oh
what the hell ..." Fortifying myself for battle, I poured
myself a little Chardonnay. Something French. Something
that says I may be white, but I can kick.

*She storms to the end of her*
*dock, waving at ARTHUR.*

MAUREEN
YOU! COPPER!

*MAUREEN points just off the tip of her dock.*

Here. I wanna talk!

ARTHUR
Oh oh. This can't be good. (*singing to himself*) "Should I
stay or should I go ..."

> *Taking a deep breath,* ARTHUR
> *moves closer.* MAUREEN *waits, like*
> *a panther waiting to pounce.*

ARTHUR
There she was, in all her glory, waving her wine
glass around like it was a samurai sword, but never
spilling a drop.

MAUREEN
It would be so easy. Just one well-aimed wine glass.

> *They stare at each other for a moment.*

ARTHUR
I'm sorry for your ...

MAUREEN
YOU LITTLE SHIT!

ARTHUR
You're grieving. This is not ...

MAUREEN
I'm grieving?! Yes I'm grieving. Over my husband. Over
my shoreline. What have I got to celebrate?

ARTHUR

Did you call me over here to fight?

MAUREEN

You realize I now have one hundred percent of my time to devote to you and all this.

ARTHUR

Ms. Poole ...

MAUREEN

Mrs. Poole. It's still Mrs. Poole.

ARTHUR

Is this what you really want to do? Right here? Right now?

MAUREEN

Why not?! Are there other cottagers you need to annoy right now? Do I have to make an appointment?

ARTHUR

No appointment necessary. You say you mourn over this lake ... I've met people like you before – you want a perfect, immaculate lake, like the ones I am sure you have on a calendar in your kitchen. You want a purely aesthetic body of water, not a productive, practical, natural one. I bet I know exactly what's going through that two-hundred-dollar haircut and tinted head of yours. "Wild rice is fine. It's great. Let the Native people do what they want, just not here, just not in my lake." A classic case of NIMBL.

MAUREEN

NIMBL? What's that?

ARTHUR

"Not In My Back Lake." I am sure deep inside you don't
hate Native people or wild rice per se, just as long as it and
we don't interfere in your life. That's why we were put on
reserves, right?

MAUREEN

Let me ask you a question. In your own community, are
there people there who are suspicious of your adherence
to your so-called traditional beliefs? Some, I discovered,
are just as traditional as you claim to be, but they don't
seem to like what you're doing either. They feel this
wild rice is sacred and should only be harvested and
raised for local consumption. Marketing and selling it
commercially demeans it.

ARTHUR

That would be Smiley, Dakota, and probably Sidney.

MAUREEN

And do I have to point out that there are many other
Native people who are not so supportive of what you're
doing? Seems some Otter Lake people, your people, have
leased lands to white cottagers who don't want your wild
rice off their shore either.

ARTHUR

Todd, Camille, and Janine. Family stuff.

**MAUREEN**

This is bigger than your family. The Kings, over by the
bridge, they want to sell their cottage but most of the
offers are a joke. Your wild rice is difficult to swim, fish,
or boat through. And you're profiting at our expense.

*MAUREEN defiantly takes a sip of her wine.*
*ARTHUR sips his Tim Hortons Ice Capp.*

**ARTHUR**

I'm sorry ... did you use the word "profit"? If I'm lucky ...
and its looking like I am increasingly going to be unlucky,
I'll barely earn enough to make it above the poverty line.
Something Indigenous is in your way, you just push it
aside. What I am doing is something you can't understand.
It involves culture. History. Heritage. I am sorry if
the celebration of our Anishnawbe culture is a slight
inconvenience for you.

**MAUREEN**

Just imagine if I dropped anchor just off your shores
and started planting God-knows-what right there in
front of you.

**ARTHUR**

Like a cottage?!

**MAUREEN**

When you own a cottage, then complain to me about
them. I am sure there are unpopulated lakes somewhere
where you can do your thing. My husband and I spent

a lot of money on this property and this cottage. This
is where we had planned to retire. Afterwards we were
planning to leave it to Cameron and Terri-Lynn to do with
as they see fit, and should there be grandchildren someday,
to them. Let me just point out that you, one single man,
are doing things that are having detrimental effects for
well over two hundred, maybe three hundred other people.
That's awfully selfish, don't you think.

*ARTHUR measures her question for a moment.*

ARTHUR
*Gaawiin.*

MAUREEN
And just what does that mean?

ARTHUR
No. I am not selfish. Add this to your list of facts.
My daughter had diabetes. Do you know why? All the
pop and chips and French fries that have flooded our
communities. KFC and ice cream and Spam and sugar
and everything else. One in four in our community have
some form of diabetes. I've got aunts and cousins missing
body parts.

MAUREEN
I am sorry to hear that, but again, I had nothing to do with
that. You're just complicating the issue ...

ARTHUR
We never had all those diseases when we ate wild meat
and *manoomin*. I'm doing this for Marie. To give her and
everybody else in our community an option. A window
to health. Again, food sovereignty. I'm doing it to increase
the chance that girls and boys like my daughter will not
have to shoot up every day with insulin. As for your
property values and boating problems, tell your first-world
problems to a member of another marginalized people.

MAUREEN
What does ...

ARTHUR
She might still be alive if I had fed her better.

MAUREEN
Alive?

ARTHUR
Diabetic ketoacidosis. Her body produced too much
ketones, something to do with not enough insulin.
I honestly believe if I had kept her away from all that
processed food, she'd still be paddling my canoe with me.

MAUREEN
When?

ARTHUR
Two years ago.

*They stare at each other. Water can
be heard lapping against Arthur's
boat and Maureen's dock.*

MAUREEN

I'm so sorry.

ARTHUR

So am I. I remember the last time Marie and I went out
in this canoe. She tried so hard to paddle with me, but
by then she had no energy. Instead, I told her to let her
fingers trail in the water. To feel the lake. To share her
spirit with the water around her. As we made our way
through the *manoomin*, her hands played with the tall
stalks, almost playing them like strings on a harp. Out
there, I shared with her ... her last teaching ... about
acceptance ...

MAUREEN

Then as quickly as he came, he turned and paddled away.
Of course I knew nothing about his daughter's medical
problems. That is so tragic. I lost my husband but the
thought of losing one of my children ... (*pause*) So I sat
here, on the dock, way into the night.

   I thought about Mr. Copper's daughter, and the
absurdity of life. I may have mentioned that I once was
a practicing Buddhist, something I'd been introduced
to in university. At the time it was what I was looking
for and what I needed to chart the path of motherhood,
being a wife, and dealing with the insanity of HR. It gave
me something to hold on to. To guide me. Until this

whole thing with Justin and Mr. Copper. One of its main teachings has to do with acceptance. Of good and bad. That's when I lost interest. And as you may have noticed, I am not very good with acceptance. I will not calmly accept my husband's death. Or that wild rice. Acceptance ... That means giving in. I will not go gentle into that good night. Or anything I believe is unfair. I need to fight. That is what makes me wake up in the morning.

But the next day I made an anonymous donation to the diabetic pediatric charity at my hospital.

*Beat.*

But that still doesn't justify what he's doing to this lake or to us. I just hope he's not using his daughter to justify his actions.

*ARTHUR gets in his canoe again.*

ARTHUR
I didn't want to tell poor Ms. Poole that basically, the cottagers had already lost the war. At least half the *manoomin* I gather goes to other Native communities that have the exact same idea I have. *Manoomin* is being planted all across the country again. And the local university and college have contacted me about including what I do in their Indigenous studies courses. Next year they've offered to help me plant and gather *manoomin* all over these bodies of water. And I will teach them how to cherish and process it. This is all going to happen in an Indigenous way.

MAUREEN

There were three lawyers with cottages on that lake, not to mention on the surrounding lakes. And Louise Richard's brother runs a rather successful public relations firm. This is the twenty-first century. We will use twenty-first century weapons to fight. I think Justin would be happy. My poor Justin, supportive as he was, thought I was tilting at windmills. He knows this is my fight. Ever since he left us I noticed I have trouble with my tenses. I keep flipping back between present and past tense. Justin likes this ... Justin liked this ... Part of me thinks he's still here. My grammar just refuses to acknowledge his death.

*For a moment, ARTHUR picks up the rice sticks and does a soft ballet with them, like he's imitating Marie. Taking a deep breath, he gets back into his canoe and begins to paddle. He seems more reflective.*

ARTHUR

One evening, when I was out in my canoe, just enjoying Starling Lake, I noticed Ms. Poole wasn't home. People had been saying she'd spread the ashes of her husband on the land there. For my daughter, I had spread her ashes in a bed of *manoomin* on this lake. Her spirit name is *Siginaakoons*, it means "Little Starling." I thought it was appropriate. It was the same *manoomin* bed I saved from the dredger. Anyway, I felt the woman's loss. So, in respect, I put some *sammon* down along her shoreline. For him. And my daughter.

It's a Native thing. How.

*Lights go down.*

*End of play.*

## ACKNOWLEDGMENTS

I wish I could say this play and everything within its universe was my idea alone. But not only would that be a bald-faced lie, as opposed to a hairy-faced one, it would also be a gross dereliction of responsibility to those who helped me carve out this play. Many people, past and present, have their fingerprints all over this creation. To those hovering in the mists of time, I would like to thank all who have told me stories over the years, all of which helped hone my ability to weave a tale or two. I constantly get asked by students where I get my ideas ... well, I get them from other stories and storytellers.

More directly, I would like to thank my mother who, for reasons of her own, decided I would be a good child to conceive and raise. I know I am rather biased on the topic, but good decision, Mom.

*Cottagers and Indians* ... this is a play I never planned to write. Even though I live at ground zero for the whole issue, I couldn't see the forest for the trees. It took Richard Rose, artistic director of Tarragon Theatre, to see the obvious, and coax me into writing it. Good decision, Richard.

An enormous thank you goes out to James Whetung. Though Arthur Copper is an invention of my own, I cannot deny that much of James's DNA runs through the play and the character. I like to think the play is a third James, a third my-own-wacky take on life, and a third sheer imagination.

Without James's struggle, this play would be a lot shorter. Keep fighting the fight, James.

It would be remiss of me to not acknowledge the contribution of the Save Pigeon Lake organization, and other people not necessarily affiliated directly with SPL, for disagreeing with James's viewpoint on wild rice. Without them there would be a lot less drama, and quite probably no play or book. So thumbs up, gang, I do deeply thank you.

And of course, Ms. Patti Shaughnessy, director and friend. Together we put this play on stage and to our joint surprise, it was a hit. A big hit. As I write this, it is going on a province-wide tour, and next year, possibly a national tour. A fellow Curve Laker, she knew James, the issue, me, and how to make wild rice seem interesting and exciting. *Chi-miigwech*, Patti.

Some additional words of thanks: to Leanne Betasamosake Simpson for permission to reprint "Land & Reconciliation: Having the Right Conversations," to Jonathon Taylor (yes, a cousin) who provided the Anishnawbe translations and helped the cast with pronunciations, and to the amazing cast and crew who made the play equally amazing. Just as important, thanks to Janine Willie, who still laughs at my jokes.

# AFTERWORD

## Land & Reconciliation: Having the Right Conversations

by LEANNE BETASAMOSAKE SIMPSON

A few summers ago, a conflict occurred between cottagers and Mississauga Nishnaabeg wild rice harvesters on Pigeon Lake when folks from the "Save Pigeon Lake" group were issued permits from the Trent-Severn Waterway and Parks Canada to hire a contractor to remove wild rice from the lake.

Curve Lake First Nation member James Whetung was at the centre of the controversy, as a harvester who sells Black Duck Wild Rice regularly at the Peterborough Farmers' Market and who has been reseeding Pigeon Lake for the past few years.

James is an important person in Mississauga Nishnaabeg communities because he is an expert on wild rice. He has spent years refining the complicated processing of the rice, nurturing the beds back to life, and teaching others how to do the same. He also provides local Nishnaabe communities, my community, and the broader Peterborough community with a local, sustainably harvested source of wild rice, so we don't have to rely on commercially produced rice from Minnesota.

*Manoomin,* or wild rice, has grown in our territory since time immemorial and it used to cover many of the lakes in this area, including Pimadashkodeyong (Rice Lake) and Chemong. Curve Lake Elder Doug Williams recounts stories of a tiny canoe path up the centre of Chemong because the rice was so thick and healthy. Our families lived good lives with a beautiful, sustainable food system because of wild rice.

*Manoomin* is a cornerstone of Mississauga Nishnaabeg governance, economy, and well-being. As a food, it is high in protein, and through a complex drying and curing process, it can last through the winter as a staple food, when hunting and fishing are more difficult. Mississauga Nishnaabeg families gather in ricing areas in the fall to pick and process rice – which involves drying, roasting, dancing, and winnowing. Songs, stories, and ceremonies are interwoven with each step. In the past, large amounts of *manoomin* were cached for the winter.

In November, wild rice harvesters from Curve Lake First Nation (Doug Williams and James Whetung) and Alderville First Nation (Dave Mowat and myself) came together with a supportive audience in the Peterborough Public Library to talk about *manoomin* and reconciliation.

Reconciliation is a word that we've heard a lot lately in the media. The Truth and Reconciliation Commission recently concluded its work and has released its final report with ninety-three recommendations, which Prime Minister Trudeau has promised to implement "in order to redress the legacy of residential schools and advance the process of Canadian reconciliation."

Land is not mentioned in any of the recommendations, in part because the commission was set up to focus on individual suffering in residential schools. Yet residential schools were a strategy used by Canada to break the connection between Indigenous Peoples and our lands, so the state could access the land for settlement and for natural resources.

By taking our children and holding them hostage, the federal government truncated what Indigenous parents were willing to do to resist the most devastating aspects of colonialism. By breaking the intimate connection between children and their families, their culture, their language, and their land, the state was attempting to assimilate Indigenous Peoples into Canadian society and eliminate barriers to natural resources and land. By removing children from Indigenous education systems, the state was hoping to eliminate Indigenous forms of governance and leadership.

Beyond the individual suffering of Indigenous children and families, residential schools have had significant, ongoing implications for maintaining the system of settler-colonialism in Canada. While colonialism is something from the past for most Canadians, Indigenous Peoples experience it as a system and a process in the present that prevents us for living as Nishnaabeg in our homeland.

Residential schools were just one part of an ugly and ongoing strategy to destroy Indigenous Nations that included policies such as the Indian Act, fraudulent treaty processes and land theft, the criminalization of Indigenous dissent and resistance, gender violence, and racism.

The past two hundred years have not been kind or fair to the Mississauga Nishnaabeg or our rice. We have been dispossessed, often violently, of virtually all of our territory, which spans the north shore of Lake Ontario.

This makes it very difficult for us to live as Nishnaabeg in our homeland.

Wild rice beds have been catastrophically destroyed through construction of the Trent-Severn Waterway and fluctuating water levels, the decline of water quality in the lakes, boat traffic, and cottagers actively removing the beds from the waterfront. Our sacred sites, our cemeteries, our hunting grounds, traplines, fishing spots, ceremonial places, camping places, trails, medicine gathering spots, and wild rice beds are very difficult to access because they are on private land, in provincial parks, or under the control of municipalities and cities.

This presents a tremendous problem for people like me who are raising Nishnaabeg children and who want our kids to fall in love with their land, know their stories and language, and live in the world as Nishnaabeg. I want them to be able to ice-fish in the winter, fast at the Kinomaage-Waapkong (the Peterborough Petroglyphs), make maple sugar and trap muskrats in the spring, hunt bullfrogs in the summer, and hunt deer, ducks, and geese, and of course harvest *manoomin* in the fall.

How can we "advance the process of Canadian reconciliation" without talking about land? Local First Nations are currently engaged in several battles to protect land: the ability to harvest rice; the burial mounds on "private land" in Hastings, Ontario; the Fraser property, a tract of land set for condo development in Burleigh Falls; and the protection of our beloved Chi'Minis/Boyd Island.

There are very few places left where we can be Nishnaabeg on our own terms. The federal and provincial governments, after years of court battles, have finally recognized hunting and fishing rights for the Williams Treaty communities. This is a tremendous victory for us, as we have very few places we can hunt. Giving these places back is an excellent start to an ongoing process of reconciliation that is more than just apologies and superficial changes.

Land is an important conversation for Indigenous Peoples and Canada to have because land is at the root of our conflicts. Far from asking settler Canadians to pack up and leave, it is critical that we think about how we can better share land. That's a conversation we're not having, except when conflict escalates to the level it did last summer on Pigeon Lake.

The night at the Peterborough Public Library showed me that there are organizations and people in the Peterborough area that are interested in figuring out how to share and protect land, and that don't feel angry or threatened about me being Nishnaabeg in my territory. Indeed, while Mississauga Nishnaabeg experience a lot of anger, racism, and violence from our neighbours, many local people have also encouraged me to hunt on their land, launch canoes from their waterfront, or harvest medicine for their bush – land that they recognize as Nishnaabeg.

I get asked "What do you people want anyway?" a lot in my travels. During Idle No More, I decided to think about that question in a deep way and commit to clearly articulating what I want as an Nishnaabekwe. At the end of my presentation that night at the library, I read my vision for the first time in the city I live in:

I want my great-grandchildren to be able to fall in love with every piece of our territory. I want their bodies to carry with them every story, every song, every piece of poetry hidden in our Nishnaabeg language. I want them to be able to dance through their lives with joy. I want them to live without fear because they know respect, because they know in their bones what respect feels like. I want them to live without fear because they have a pristine environment with clean waterways that will provide them with the physical and emotional sustenance to uphold their responsibilities to the land, their families, their communities, and their nations. I want them to be valued, heard, and cherished by our communities and by Canada no matter their skin colour, their physical and mental abilities, their sexual orientation, or their gender.

I want my great-great-grandchildren and their great-great-grandchildren to be able to live as Mississauga Nishnaabeg, unharassed and undeterred in our homeland.

The idea of my arms embracing my grandchildren, and their arms embracing their grandchildren is communicated in the Nishnaabe word *kobade*. According to Elder Edna Manitowabi, *kobade* is a word we use to refer to our great grandparents and our great-grandchildren. It means "a link in a chain" – a link in the chain between generations, between nations, between states of being, between individuals. I am a link in a chain. We are all links in a chain.

Doug Williams, a Mississauga Nishnaabeg Elder from Curve Lake First Nation, calls our nation *Kina Gchi Nishnaabeg-ogamig* – "the place where we all live and work together." Our nation is a hub of Nishnaabe networks. It is a long *kobade*, cycling through time. It is a web of connections to each other, to the plant nations, the animal nations, the rivers and lakes, the cosmos, and our neighbouring Indigenous nations.

*Kina Gchi Nishnaabeg-ogamig* is an ecology of intimacy. It is an ecology of relationships in the absence of coercion, hierarchy, or authoritarian power.

*Kina Gchi Nishnaabeg-ogamig* is connectivity based on the sanctity of the land, the love we have for our families, our language, our way of life. It is relationships based on deep reciprocity, respect, non-interference, self-determination, and freedom.

Our nationhood is based on the idea that the earth is our first mother, that "natural resources" are not "natural resources" at all, but gifts from our mother. Our nationhood is based on the foundational concept that we should give up what we can to support the integrity of our homelands for the coming generations. We should give more than we take.

It is nationhood based on a series of radiating responsibilities.

This is what I understand our diplomats were negotiating when settlers first arrived in our territory. This was the impetus for those very first treaties – Nishnaabe freedom, protection for the land and the environment, a space – an intellectual, political, spiritual, artistic, creative, and physical space where we could live as Nishnaabe and where our *kobade* could do the same.

This is what my Ancestors wanted for me, for us. They wanted for our generation to practice Nishnaabe governance over our homeland, to partner with other governments over shared lands, to have the ability to make decisions about how the gifts of our mother would be used for the benefit of our people and in a manner to promote her sanctity for coming generations. I believe my ancestors expected the settler state to recognize my nation, our lands, and the political and cultural norms in our territory.

My nationhood doesn't just radiate outwards, it also radiates inwards. It is my physical body, my mind, and my spirit. It is our families – not the nuclear family that has been normalized in settler society, but big, beautiful, diverse, extended multiracial families of relatives and friends that care very deeply for each other.

If reconciliation is to be meaningful, we need to be willing to dismantle settler-colonialism as a system. Our current government needs to move beyond window dressing and begin to tackle the root causes of Indigenous oppression in Canada. This means respecting when Indigenous Peoples say no to development on our lands. It means dismantling land claims and self-government processes that require us to terminate our Aboriginal and Treaty Rights to sit at the table. It means repealing the most damaging aspects of the Indian Act and respecting First Nations political systems, governance, and ability to determine who belongs in our communities. It means being accountable about the collective damage that has been done and is being done, and supporting the regeneration of languages, cultures, and political systems. It means stop fighting us in court. It means giving back land, so we can rebuild and recover from the losses of the last four centuries and truly enter into a new relationship with Canada and Canadians.

This article was first published online by *Electric City Magazine*, and is reproduced with the author's kind permission.

DREW HAYDEN TAYLOR is an award-winning playwright, novelist, essayist, and filmmaker. Born on the Curve Lake First Nation in Central Ontario, Drew has done practically everything from performing stand-up comedy at the John F. Kennedy Center for the Performing Arts in Washington, DC, to serving as artistic director for Canada's premiere Indigenous theatre company, Native Earth Performing Arts, in Toronto. Somehow, in the midst of that, he's managed to carve out time to write the occasional story. *Cottagers and Indians* is his thirty-second book.